THE PANTILES.
TUNBRIDGE WELLS.

FAVOURITE KENTISH RECIPES

compiled by
Pat Smith

with illustrations
by A.R. Quinton

SALMON

*I*NDEX

Cover pictures: *front* Smallhythe near Tenterden; *back* Cottage at Frogholt

Printed and Published by J. Salmon Ltd., Sevenoaks, England ©

Kentish Huffkins

1 lb. strong bread flour
2 oz. lard
2 teaspoons sugar
1 teaspoon salt
½ oz. fresh yeast
½ pint milk and water mixed

Eat as bread rolls or fill the 'hole' with fruit or jam and top with a little whipped cream.

Sieve the flour into a warm bowl. Rub the lard into the flour and add the salt and the sugar. Leave in a warm place for a few minutes. Heat the milk/water until tepid; crumble the fresh yeast into the liquid and stir until blended. Add the yeast mixture to the dry ingredients and mix well. Turn on to a floured surface and knead until smooth. Return to the bowl, cover and leave in a warm place until doubled in size (about 1 hour). Divide the dough into 12 pieces. Roll into round balls and place on a greased, floured baking sheet. Leave room between rolls for expansion. Press a floured finger into the centre of each roll to form a hole. Leave in the warm to rise for 20 minutes. Set oven to 425°F or Mark 7 and bake for 20 minutes until risen and golden brown.

PENSHURST PLACE & CHURCH

A.R.QUINTON

Penshurst Place and Church

KENTISH WELL PUDDING

8 oz, self-raising flour
2 oz. fresh breadcrumbs
4 oz. shredded suet
Pinch of salt
6 oz. currants
4 oz. butter
4 oz. brown sugar
Grated rind of 1 lemon
A little milk and water

Mix the flour, breadcrumbs, suet and salt and make into a fairly soft dough with a mixture of milk and water. Roll out threequarters of the dough and use it to line a greased 2 pint basin. Press the currants into the pastry lining. Cream the butter, sugar and lemon rind and form into a ball. Roll out the remaining pastry and enclose the 'butter ball' in it, sealing the pastry around it. Place the whole ball in the lined basin. Draw the outer pastry over the top of the ball. Cover with greased paper and a cloth or foil. Steam for 3 hours. Serve with custard. Serves 5 to 6.

Traditionally this pudding would have been cooked in a cloth

CHERRY ALMOND SHORTCAKE

6 oz. shortcrust pastry
1 oz. glacé cherries
1 oz. margarine
2 oz. caster sugar
4 oz. ground almonds
Almond essence
1 egg, beaten

Set oven to 375°F or Mark 5. Roll out the pastry and use to line a sandwich or flan tin, approximately 6½ inches diameter. Place the cherries on the base of the pastry case. Cream the margarine and the sugar. Add the almonds and finally the egg, mixed with a few drops of the essence. Spread the mixture over the cherries and bake for 10 minutes, then reduce the heat to 350°F or Mark 4 for a further 10 minutes. Cool in the tin, then cut into squares.

Appledore Chicken Pie

1 chicken, or joints, to give 1½ lbs.
of raw chicken meat
2 hard boiled eggs, sliced
2 or 3 rashers of bacon, de-rinded
and chopped
1 tablespoon fresh herbs, finely chopped
or 1 teaspoon dried herbs
Salt and pepper
1½ oz. flour
8 oz. shortcrust pastry

Set oven to 375°F or Mark 5. Remove the chicken meat from the bones. Place the bones in a pan, cover with water, put on a lid and simmer for 2–3 hours to produce some stock. Roll the meat in seasoned flour and put a layer in a pie dish. Cover with the chopped bacon and egg slices. Finish with the remaining chicken. Sprinkle the herbs over the meat. Cover with a pastry lid, making a hole in the centre and bake for 1 hour. Reduce the temperature to 350°F or Mark 4 and cook for a further 1 hour. If the pastry appears to be browning too rapidly, protect with a piece of greaseproof paper. Remove from the oven and, through the hole in the pastry, top up with some of the hot stock from the bones. Serves 4.

Kentish Pan Cake

3 eggs
2 whites of egg
¼ pint milk
¼ pint double cream
2 tablespoons sherry
3 dessertspoons brandy
4 oz. flour
A pinch of powdered ginger
A pinch of salt
Grated nutmeg to taste
1 tablespoon caster sugar
½ medium sized cooking apple
Lard for frying

Put the eggs and the extra egg whites, milk, cream, sherry, brandy, flour, salt and the spices in a mixing bowl. Beat well until smooth. Peel and core the apple and chop it finely. Add the sugar and apple to the batter and leave to stand in a cool place for 30 minutes. Lightly grease the frying pan with the lard, fry the pancakes and stack them on a large piece of greaseproof paper. Then wrap them in the paper and keep warm until needed. Turn the 'stack' on to a warm plate and dredge with icing sugar. Cut into wedges and serve with whipped cream and puréed apple. Serves 6.

Brenchley Village

L_{AMB} P_{IE}

1 lb. fillet of lamb
6 oz. gooseberries
4 oz. spinach or cos lettuce
Pepper and salt
Nutmeg
Blade of mace
5 tablespoons chicken or
vegetable stock
8 oz. shortcrust pastry

Set oven to 375°F or Mark 5. Grease an 8 inch (approx.) pie dish. Cut the meat into small pieces and place them in the dish. Season with salt, pepper and nutmeg. Lay the blade of mace on top of the meat. Scald the spinach (or lettuce) in boiling water for 1 minute, then lay it on top of the meat. Finally make a layer of gooseberries. Pour on the stock. Cover the pie with a pastry lid and make a hole in the centre. Bake for 1 hour, then cover the pastry with greaseproof paper to protect it. Reduce the temperature to 325°F or Mark 3 and bake for a further 1¾ hours. Serves 4.

GINGER COB-NUT CAKE

8 oz. self-raising flour
1 rounded teaspoon powdered ginger
4 oz. margarine
4 oz. brown sugar
2 oz. Kentish cob-nuts, roasted, skinned and chopped
1 large egg, beaten

Set oven to 350°F or Mark 4. Sift the flour and the ginger into a bowl. Rub in the margarine until the mixture resembles breadcrumbs. Add the sugar and the nuts. Mix in the beaten egg, keeping the mixture crumbly. Turn into a greased tin approximately 9 inches by 4 inches and bake for 20 minutes. Cool in the tin and cut into squares.

Shakespeare Cliff, Dover

*D*OVER *S*OLE *with watercress and anchovy butter*

8 fillets of sole, skinned
A bunch of watercress
2 oz. unsalted butter, softened
1 teaspoon anchovy essence
½ lemon

Set oven to 350°F or Mark 4. Grease an ovenproof dish. Season the fillets with pepper and lemon juice, then roll each one up and place side by side, join side down, in the dish. Sprinkle with a little more lemon juice, then cover with greased foil. Cook in the oven for 15–20 minutes. Meanwhile trim the watercress, reserving a few sprigs for garnish, and blanch in boiling water for 1 minute. Refresh it under cold water, then drain it. Chop the cress finely and blend with the butter and anchovy essence. This can be done in a blender. Form into 8 'pats' and leave in a cool place until needed. Place the cooked fillets on a warm dish, garnish with the reserved sprigs of watercress and serve with the pats of watercress butter. Serves 4.

Oat Biscuits

4 oz. butter
4 oz. brown sugar
6 oz. rolled oats
6 oz. flour
1 teaspoon bicarbonate of soda
2 tablespoons milk

Set oven to 300°F or Mark 2. Cream the butter and the sugar in a bowl. Mix in the oats and sift the flour and the bicarbonate of soda together into the mixture and mix thoroughly. Add enough milk to form the mixture into a dough. Roll out the dough thinly and cut into rounds with a 2 inch cutter. Bake for approximately 20 minutes or until golden brown. Makes 36 biscuits.

FOLKESTONE PUDDING PIE

8 oz. shortcrust pastry
¾ oz. ground rice
½ pint milk
Grated rind of a lemon
1 oz. butter
1 tablespoon sugar
1 egg, beaten
2 oz. currants
A little grated nutmeg

Set oven to 400°F or Mark 6. Roll out the pastry and use it to line a greased 7 inch flan tin. Mix the ground rice with a little of the cold milk. Heat the rest of the milk in a saucepan, with the lemon rind, over a low heat. Add the butter and the rice mixture to the hot milk. Stir until to thickens. Add the sugar and stir until it has dissolved. Cool slightly and whisk in the egg. Pour the mixture into the pastry case and scatter the currants on the surface. Top with a little grated nutmeg. Bake for 10 minutes and then reduce the temperature to 300°F or Mark 2 and bake for a further 20 minutes until golden and set. Serves 5 to 6.

CHERRY BRANDY

Morello cherries
Brandy
Caster sugar
Cloves (optional)

The cherries should be gathered in dry weather. Wipe them with a dry cloth and remove the stalks. Prick the fruit with a darning needle and three-quarters fill wide-necked bottles. Add sugar to the fruit, allowing 3 oz. of sugar to every 1 lb. of fruit. Top up each bottle with brandy; if desired, 3 or 4 cloves may be added to each bottle before securing the top. Keep for 2 months before using, shaking occasionally.

College Gate and All Saints Church, Maidstone

Savoury Puffs

1 small onion
2 small mushrooms
1 dessertspoon oil or butter
½ lb. mashed potatoes
2 oz. self-raising flour
1 yolk of egg
Salt and pepper

FILLING
2 oz. cooked minced meat
2 teaspoons mushroom ketchup or
Worcestershire sauce

Cook the onion and the mushrooms in the oil until softened. Add this mixture, with the flour, egg yolk and the seasoning, to the mashed potato and blend thoroughly into a dry dough. Roll it out to ¼ inch thickness. Cut the dough into 6 rounds. Mix the meat with the ketchup and put a teaspoonful on each round. Draw the potato up around the filling and seal. Flatten slightly and fry until golden brown on both sides. Serves 2.

Thatched House Pudding

2 oz. butter
4 tablespoons flour
1 pint of milk
Rind and juice of 1 lemon
Sugar to taste
3 eggs, separated
2 tablespoons hot apricot jam
1 tablespoon roasted almonds

Set oven to 375°F or Mark 5. Melt the butter in a saucepan and add the flour. Cook for 2 minutes without browning, then leave to cool slightly. Return to the heat and gradually add the milk, stirring continuously, until it boils and thickens. Remove from the heat and beat in the rind and juice of the lemon, the sugar and the egg yolks. Leave to cool. Beat the egg whites until stiff and gently fold into the sauce mixture, using a metal spoon. Pour into a well-buttered 2 pint pie dish. Bake for 20 to 25 minutes until it is well risen and golden. Remove from the oven, pour the hot jam over and top with the almonds. Serve immediately. Serves 5 to 6.

Warning: Do not open the oven door whilst the pudding is cooking or it will sink.

THE HARBOUR, WHISTABLE

A.R.QUINTON

The Harbour, Whitstable

Whitstable Angels on Horseback

Oysters
1 rasher smoked bacon for
each oyster
Buttered toast

Remove the oysters from their shells. Wrap each oyster in a rasher of bacon. Put them on a skewer and grill them until the bacon is cooked. Alternatively, they can be cooked in a hot oven. Serve piping hot on buttered toast.

STRAWBERRY TARTLETS

8 oz. strawberries, sliced
2 oz. caster sugar
2 eggs
4 oz. shortcrust pastry

Set oven to 375°F or Mark 5. Mix the sliced berries with the sugar. Roll out the pastry and use it to line some tartlet tins. Whisk the eggs and blend with the fruit mixture. Three-quarters fill each tart case with the strawberry mixture. Bake for 12 to 15 minutes.

APRICOT CREAM CAKES

4 oz. butter
4 oz. caster sugar
1 egg
4 oz. self-raising flour
3 teaspoons fairly thick apricot jam
2 tablespoons thick cream

Set oven to 350°F or Mark 4. Cream the butter and sugar in a bowl and beat in the egg. Fold in the sifted flour and finally fold in the jam and the cream, gently. Drop small quantities (about 1 teaspoon) on to a greased baking sheet. Give them plenty of space as they will spread. Bake for approximately 10–15 minutes until golden brown.

Kentish Apple and Cheese Pie

6 oz. puff or shortcrust pastry
1½ lbs. cooking apples, peeled, cored and thickly sliced
3–4 oz. granulated sugar
3–4 cloves
Small pinch of grated nutmeg
½ tea cup of water
4 oz. hard cheese, sliced

Set oven to 425°F or Mark 7. Using half the apples, put a layer into a greased 8 inch (approx.) pie dish. Sprinkle half the sugar over the apples. Lay the remaining apples on top and push the cloves into some of the apple slices. Add the remaining sugar, the nutmeg and the water and make a final layer with the cheese. Roll out the pastry and use it to cover the dish. Brush with a little milk and bake for approximately 40–45 minutes. Serves 4–6.

High Street, Biddenden

White Vegetable Soup

8 oz. potatoes
8 oz. carrots
8 oz. onions
8 oz. turnips
4 sticks of celery
1 level tablespoon butter or oil
Salt and pepper
½ pint of milk
1½ pints water or chicken or vegetable stock
1 oz. spaghetti (broken into small pieces)
1 tablespoon chopped parsley

Wash and peel the vegetables. Cut them into fine dice. Melt the fat in a saucepan over a low heat and sweat the vegetables in it for 10 minutes. Add the water, or stock, and the seasoning and bring to the boil. Simmer for 1 hour by which time the vegetables should be tender. Add the spaghetti and the milk. Simmer for a further 15 minutes. Serve in bowls or a tureen with the parsley sprinkled on the surface. Serves 4 to 5.

Kipper Savoury

2 kippers, filleted
2 oz. butter
Pepper
1 dessertspoon anchovy essence
1 generous teaspoon mushroom ketchup
2 tablespoons double cream
1 tablespoon flaked almonds, fried or roasted
2 slices wholemeal toast

Pound the flesh from the kippers together with the butter, anchovy essence, mushroom ketchup and the cream or mix until well blended in a food processor. Spread on wholemeal toast and decorate with the almonds.

The addition of the anchovy essence and mushroom ketchup in this recipe is very much according to personal taste and will be dictated by the saltiness of the kippers.

Canterbury Cathedral

Pork and Apple Pudding

1 lb. self-raising flour
A pinch of salt
8 oz. shredded suet
Water to mix
1½ lb. raw pork, cut into small pieces
Chopped sage to taste
1 large cooking apple, peeled, cored and sliced
Salt and pepper

Sieve the flour and the salt into a bowl and add the suet. Mix to a soft dough with some water. Use threequarters of the pastry to line a greased 2½ pint pudding basin. Put layers of the meat and apple alternately in the lined basin and season well with the sage, salt and pepper. Close the pudding with a lid, using the remaining pastry. Fold the edges of the lining back over the edge of the lid; this will help to seal it. Cover with greased paper and a cloth or foil. Steam for 4 hours. Serves 5 to 6.

Wassail Bowl

1 quart ale
½ bottle sherry
1 teaspoon freshly grated nutmeg
1 teaspoon ground ginger
1 teaspoon ground cinnamon
2 slices of toast
Juice and rind of 1 lemon
2 medium sized baked apples, chopped
Sugar to taste
1 orange

Mix all the ingredients in a large saucepan. Heat the mixture but *do not* let it boil. Allow to stand for 1 hour. Strain and re-heat. Serve either in a large bowl with slices of orange floating on the surface or in individual mugs or tumblers each with a slice of orange. If using glass tumblers make sure that the mixture is not too hot.

This Old English punch is an ideal and warming drink after Carol Singing.

CRANBROOK CHERRY AND ALMOND PIE

1 lb. cherries
1 egg
The weight of the egg in each of the following ingredients:
Butter
Caster sugar
Self-raising flour
Ground almonds

A few drops of almond essence

Set oven to 350°F or Mark 4. Wash and de-stalk the cherries. Grease a shallow ovenproof dish and place the cherries in it. Cream the butter and the sugar together. Beat in the egg, then fold in the flour, almonds and the essence. Spread the mixture over the fruit and place in the oven for approximately 20–25 minutes or until the mixture is risen and golden brown. Serve with custard or cream. Serves 2 to 3

Roman Pie

1 lb. puff pastry
1 rabbit or small chicken (jointed)
1 medium sized onion
1 medium sized leek
1 medium sized carrot
2 mushrooms
1 tablespoon butter
1 pint chicken or vegetable stock
Salt and pepper
2 oz. cooked macaroni
2 oz. grated cheese
3 tablespoons single cream

Set oven to 350°F or Mark 4. Soften the onion in the butter in a saucepan and add the other vegetables. Place in a greased casserole and add the rabbit or chicken joints. Season and pour on the stock. Cover the dish and cook for approximately 1 hour or until tender. Remove from oven and leave to cool. Flake the meat from the bones. Reset the oven to 425°F or Mark 7. Roll out the pastry and line an 8 inch pie dish with part of it. Place half of the meat, vegetables, macaroni and cheese in layers in the dish, then repeat with the remaining ingredients. Pour on the liquid from the casserole with the cream and cover with a pastry lid. Make a hole in the centre of the lid. Brush with a little milk. Bake for ½ hour, lower the oven temperature to 375°F or Mark 5 and cook for a further ½ hour. Serves 4 to 5.

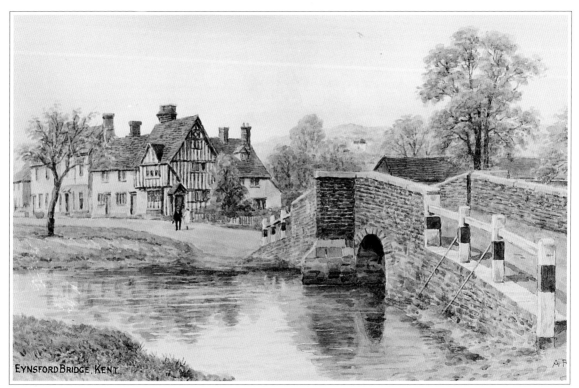

EYNSFORD BRIDGE, KENT.

A.R

The Ford and Bridge, Eynsford

Fudge Cake

½ lb. semi-sweet or digestive biscuits
(broken into small but uneven pieces)
6 oz. chopped nuts
1 rounded tablespoon cocoa
4 oz. butter
4 oz. brown sugar
1 egg, beaten

CAKE COVERING
2 oz. plain chocolate
1 teaspoon golden syrup
½ oz. butter
1 tablespoon chopped nuts

Melt the butter in a fairly large saucepan. Add the sugar, cocoa and egg and stir them over the heat until the mixture thickens. Add the biscuits and the nuts and stir well until they are coated with the mixture. Turn into two greased 7 inch sandwich tins and press down evenly. Leave in a refrigerator overnight until set. Next day melt the chocolate in a basin over hot water and stir in the syrup and butter whilst the chocolate is still warm. Mix well. Use a little of the mixture to sandwich the two cakes together; spread the rest on top to decorate. Scatter the nuts on the coating before it sets.

Tomato Pickle

5 lb. green tomatoes, sliced
Salt
1 lb. brown sugar
1 lb. onions, sliced
¼ teaspoon cayenne pepper
1 quart malt vinegar
1 oz. whole pickling spice (bruised and put into a muslin bag and tied)

Do not use brass, copper or iron utensils when making pickles. Use, instead, stainless steel, aluminium or enamelled pans and wooden spoons for stirring.

Place the sliced tomatoes in a dish with salt sprinkled between the layers. Leave overnight. Next day, rinse the tomatoes thoroughly in cold water, to remove the salt, and drain. Put into a pan with the sugar, onions, pepper and vinegar. Immerse the spices in the liquid. Bring to the boil and simmer until the tomatoes and onion are tender. Remove the spice bag. Lift out the solids with a slotted spoon and use to fill warm jars to within ¾ inch of the rim. Return the pan to the heat and reduce the liquid by a quarter to a half by boiling rapidly. Use this liquid to top up the jars, and cover with 'vinegar-proof' lids.

Central Parade and Beach, Deal

Fish Loaf

1 breakfast cupful cooked white fish
¾ breakfast cupful fresh breadcrumbs
1 tablespoon anchovy essence
2 heaped teaspoons piccalilli
1 egg
Salt and pepper

Flake the fish and remove all the skin and bones. Mix the flakes thoroughly with the essence and the liquid of the piccalilli. Chop the vegetables of the piccalilli finely before adding to the mixture. Add the breadcrumbs, the seasoning and, lastly, the egg to bind it all together. Put into a greased 1 pint basin, cover with greased paper and/or kitchen foil. Steam for 1 hour. Turn out and serve with parsley or tomato sauce. Serves 2–3.

CRAB APPLE JELLY

Crab apples
To each pound of apples:
½ inch fresh ginger
3 cloves
1 lb. sugar to every pint of juice

Cut the apples, through the cores, into pieces. Place in a pan with the ginger and the cloves and cover with water. Cook until soft. Strain through a jelly bag and allow to drip. Heat the juice and the sugar gently until the sugar is dissolved. Then boil rapidly until setting point is reached. Pot into warm jars and cover.

*V*INEGAR *C*AKE

12 oz. self-raising flour
4 oz. butter or dripping
8 oz. mixed fruit
2 oz. candied peel, cut fine
8 oz. demerara sugar
1 teaspoon mixed spice
1 teaspoon bicarbonate of soda
3 teaspoons vinegar
½ pint milk

Set oven to 350°F or Mark 4. Rub the fat into the flour until the mixture resembles fine breadcrumbs. Add the rest of the dry ingredients except the bicarbonate of soda. When well blended add the bicarbonate of soda mixed with the milk and the vinegar. Put onto a greased and lined 8½ inch cake tin and bake for approximately 1¾–2 hours.

A cake suitable for those who do not eat eggs.

'Hell' Balls

4 oz. cooked game
4 oz. cooked ham or lean, cooked bacon rashers
2 oz. chutney
Pinch of cayenne pepper
2 or 3 stoned olives, chopped
1 tablespoon game gravy
1 large egg, beaten
2 oz. (approximately) fresh white breadcrumbs

Mince the game and the ham or bacon and mix thoroughly with the chutney, cayenne pepper, olives, gravy and 1 dessertspoon of the egg. Form the mixture into 12 balls and roll them first in the remaining beaten egg and then in the breadcrumbs. Fry in shallow oil until golden brown. Serve with a side salad. Serves 2.

LEEDS CASTLE, Nr MAIDSTONE   A R QUINTON

Leeds Castle

Oast Cakes

8 oz. flour
½ teaspoon baking powder
2 oz. lard
2 oz. caster sugar
3 oz. currants
1 teaspoon lemon juice
Water or parsnip wine
(or a mixture of both)

ALTERNATIVE SUGGESTIONS
Butter instead of lard
1 level teaspoon mixed spice
(added with the dry ingredients)

Sift the flour and the baking powder into a bowl. Rub in the lard until the mixture is like breadcrumbs. Add the sugar and the currants to the mixture. Mix in the lemon juice and the water or parsnip wine until the dough is soft but not wet. Roll out thinly and cut into rounds. Fry in shallow oil until golden brown on both sides.

These were made in the hop gardens, by the pickers, for their meal breaks. They are best eaten fresh.

Filleted Plaice Savoury

4 skinned fillets of plaice
4 oz. peeled shrimps
1½ oz. butter
1 oz. fresh breadcrumbs
1 teaspoon anchovy essence
A little fish or chicken stock
1 teacup milk
1 tablespoon grated cheese

SAUCE
1 oz. butter
1 oz. flour
¼ pint milk
1 tablespoon fresh herbs

Set oven to 350°F or Mark 4. Pound the shrimps in a mortar and mix with the breadcrumbs; or chop them all in a food processor. Mix in ½ oz. of butter and essence. Melt the remaining butter in a pan. Add the shrimp mixture and moisten with a little stock. Stir until bubbling. Leave to cool. Spread the mixture evenly over each fillet. Roll them up and place, join side down, in a greased ovenproof dish; add the milk. Cover and cook for 10–15 minutes. For the sauce, melt the butter in a pan and stir in the flour. Cook for 1 minute and then cool slightly. Pour the cooked fish liquid into the pan with the extra milk and, stirring continuously, bring to the boil. Stir in the herbs and pour over the fillets. Sprinkle the cheese over the sauce and return the dish to the oven to brown. Serves 2.

High Street, Goudhurst

*W*ALNUT *L*OAF

4 oz. margarine
4 oz. caster sugar
1 beaten egg
8 oz. self-raising flour
6 oz. chopped walnuts
4 oz. sultanas
1 level teaspoon salt
¼ pint milk, approximately

Set oven to 350°F or Mark 4. Grease a 2 lb. loaf tin. In a bowl cream the margarine and the sugar. Beat in the egg. Fold in the sifted flour, nuts, sultanas and the salt. Mix in sufficient milk to make a 'dropping' consistency. Turn into the tin and bake for approximately 1 hour. Serve, cut into slices and buttered generously.

Gingerbread

2 large eggs
10 oz. black treacle or a mixture of golden syrup and treacle
3 oz. brown sugar
3 oz. margarine
8 oz. self-raising flour
1–1½ teaspoons ground ginger
½ teaspoon ground cloves
¼ teaspoon ground mace
Grated rind of 1 lemon

Set oven to 325°F or Mark 3. Heat the margarine in a pan until just melted but not too hot. Whisk the eggs until they are very frothy. Keep whisking whilst gradually adding first the treacle, then the sugar and lastly the margarine. Fold in the sifted flour, together with the spices and the lemon rind. Grease thoroughly a tin approximately 9 inches x 7 inches x 2 inches and line the base of the tin with baking parchment. Pour the mixture into the tin and bake for approximately 40 minutes. Cool on a wire rack.

LEMON PUDDING

6 oz. puff pastry
4 oz. butter
4 oz. caster sugar
Finely grated rind of 2 medium
sized lemons
Juice of 1 lemon (app. 4 tablespoons)
4 egg yolks
2 egg whites
1 tablespoon icing sugar for decoration

Set oven to 400°F or Mark 6. Line a greased sandwich tin, approximately 7 inches diameter, with very thinly rolled pastry. Cream the butter, sugar and the lemon rind together. Beat the egg yolks and whites lightly together and then whip them into the creamed mixture. Mix in the lemon juice. Turn the mixture into the pastry case and cover with a lid of thinly rolled pastry. Bake for 10 minutes then reduce the temperature to 300°F or Mark 2 and bake for a further 35 minutes. Remove from the tin and dredge with icing sugar. Serves 4 to 5.

Filo pastry could replace the puff pastry

METRIC CONVERSIONS

The weights, measures and oven temperatures used in the preceding recipes can be easily converted to their metric equivalents.

Weights

Avoirdupois	Metric
1 oz.	just under 30 grams
4 oz. (¼ lb.)	app. 115 grams
8 oz. (½ lb.)	app. 230 grams
1 lb.	454 grams

Liquid Measures

Imperial	Metric
1 tablespoon (liquid only)	20 millilitres
1 fl. oz.	app. 30 millilitres
1 gill (¼ pt.)	app. 145 millilitres
½ pt.	app. 285 millilitres
1 pt.	app. 570 millilitres
1 qt.	app. 1.140 litres

Oven Temperatures

	°Fahrenheit	Gas Mark	°Celsius
Slow	300	2	140
	325	3	158
Moderate	350	4	177
	375	5	190
	400	6	204
Hot	425	7	214
	450	8	232
	500	9	260